The Joy of Breathing

The Judaism and Modern Times Series

THE JOY
OF
BREATHING

by

Rabbi Yitzchak Ginsburgh

Gal Einai

Jerusalem • New York

The Judaism and Modern Times Series

The Joy of Breathing

Rabbi Yitzchak Ginsburgh

Edited by Yonatan Gordon (United States)
and Rachel Gordon (Israel)
Contributing Editors: Shelli Karzen and Zahava Margulis

Printed in the United States of America and Israel
First Edition

Copyright © 5780 (2020) by Gal Einai

All rights reserved. No part of this publication may be reproduced or transmitted in any form or by any means electronic or mechanical, including photocopying, recording, or any information storage and retrieval system, without written permission, except in the case of brief quotations in critical articles and reviews.

For information:

Israel: Gal Einai
           PO Box 1015
           Kfar Chabad 60840
           tel. (in Israel): 1-700-700-966
           tel. (from abroad): 972-3-9608008
email: books@inner.org
Web: www.inner.org
Twitter: @RabbiGinsburgh

Printed with the support of the Torah Institute of Yeshivat Od Yosef Chai.

Layout: David Hillel
Cover design: Heni Ben Aharon, Studio Sihara
Cover illustration: Yanky Gitlin

ISBN: 978-965-532-059-6

בברכה

"...It would be proper to publish your classes in book form.
With blessings for success..."

*– from a letter from the Lubavitcher Rebbe
to the author, Elul 5741*

Dedicated to my daughter

חדוה צפרה
Chedva Tzippora

From her father
Yonatan Gordon

TABLE OF CONTENTS

Introduction

This booklet is being compiled while the world is in the throes of a rare pandemic. The world has come to a stop. Millions of people are under lockdown. All that is left of a world that was confidently striding into a bold, technological future is one big question mark. Meditating on the significance of a universal health calamity such as this, it is natural for us to seek a spiritual perspective.

In his teachings, Rabbi Yitzchak Ginsburgh *shlit"a* offers insights into the spiritual origin of disease and healing and the knowledge necessary to reach optimal spiritual, mental and emotional health. These in turn, positively affect our physical state.

In this compilation, we have collected some of Rabbi Ginsburgh's perceptions on the immune system and the respiratory system together with a meditative breathing technique that infuses joy into our lives and connects us to the unity of the Creator.

Breathing with joy, one of the general themes of this booklet, will help us to connect to our Creator and bask in His light, enjoying good health and happiness.

The current pandemic is an opportunity for us to learn how to serve God with joy, gladness of spirit, sincerity, and wholeheartedness. With this in mind, we can significantly improve both our spiritual and physical health.

May we immediately see Mashiach, who will bring healing to the Jewish People and universal well-being, together with the true and complete redemption, which is the ultimate good for all of creation.

Yonatan Gordon (United States)
and Rachel Gordon (Israel), editors
28th of Nisan 5780

Editor's note: This is a discussion of spiritual remedies. Spirituality ultimately manifests in and influences the physical world, hence the long-term efficacy of spiritual advice. For physical ailments, please contact your medical practitioner.

1

RESPIRATORY PROBLEMS AND THEIR SPIRITUAL SOURCE

The Book of Psalms[1] concludes with the verse, "Let every soul praise God. *Hallelujah.*" In Hebrew, "soul" (נְשָׁמָה) is cognate to "breath" (נְשִׁימָה). The sages[2] interpret the verse to mean, "With every breath, praise God." One should have in mind to give thanks and praise to God with every breath he takes.[3]

Our physical breathing is an indication that at the spiritual level we are integrating Divine vitality into our souls. With every breath we take, God restores and revitalizes our spirit and bonds it with our bodies, as He did with the first man, of whom the verse states, "And He breathed into his nostrils the soul of life."[4] When an individual stops breathing, God forbid, the soul departs from his body.

With every breath we take, we can sense how God is recreating us and the world anew at every moment, as

---

1. Psalms 150:6.
2. 2 *Bereishit Rabah* 14:9; *Devarim Rabah* 2:37.
3. https://www.inner.org/torah_and_science/torah-healing/the-spiritual-side-of-respiratory-problems
4. Genesis 2:7.

taught by the Baal Shem Tov,[5] founder of the Chassidic movement. With every inhalation, we receive a Divine invitation to stand before God and connect with Him.

The intake of spiritual vitality occurs in *keter* (the *sefirah* of crown), the highest, superconscious level of the soul. For this reason, in Kabbalah and Chassidut, the entire respiratory system corresponds to *keter*.[6] By Divine Providence, the morphology of the type of virus that is causing the current pandemic resembles a halo, or tiara, and the official name chosen for the virus means "crown."

According to Kabbalah, *keter* comprises three "heads," each of which manifests as a super-conscious spiritual quality: faith, pleasure and will. This indicates that an individual suffering from respiratory problems, especially the current virus, in addition to following proper medical advice, should reinforce his faith in God, his pleasure in studying Torah and *mitzvot*, and his will to perform *mitzvot* immediately. These correspond to each of the three heads of *keter*. He should work to uproot doubts in his faith in God, take pleasure in God and not in worldly pursuits, and fulfill God's will.

Active Breathing and the Breathing Rhythm

Keter represents the unconscious level of our respiratory system. In addition, there is a level of breathing that can be consciously controlled. This aspect relates to two other

---

5.   See *Likutei Sichot* 25:200ff.
6.   *Body, Mind and Soul* p. 74.

sefirot, *binah* (the *sefirah* of understanding) and *malchut* (the *sefirah* of kingdom). *Binah* controls the breathing rhythm and *malchut* controls the depth, or capacity of the respiration process. Both of these *sefirot* are relatively "feminine."

Binah (the *sefirah* of understanding) is the higher mother figure, whose inner attribute is joy. Joy in God's service is the source of the rhythm that generates breathing.

Impaired respiratory function is one of the physical manifestations of fear, and anxiety often causes shortness of breath. In Hebrew, "lung" (רֵיאָה) is an anagram for "awe" (יִרְאָה).[7] Thus, at the spiritual level, fear of God is another vital component of rectified breathing.

The verse states, "A God-fearing woman will be praised." This is referring to the feminine "daughter" figure of *malchut* (the *sefirah* of kingdom), which is constructed from *gevurah* (the *sefirah* of might), the *sefirah* more commonly associated with fear.[8] Thus, the spiritual rectification for respiratory problems is by unifying the two parallel verses, "Serve God with joy"[9] and "Serve God with awe."[10]

The intellectual power of *binah* (the *sefirah* of understanding) is the source of the emotive powers of the soul. *Malchut* (the *sefirah* of kingdom) is the culmination of

---

7. Two other permutations of these letters are "sight" (רְאִיָּה) and "lion" (אַרְיֵה).
8. See our book in Hebrew, *Esa Einai*, p.162-163.
9. Psalms 100:2.
10. Psalms 2:11.

the emotive powers and their manifestation. The way to achieve unity between these two is to rectify the seven emotive powers of the soul by inter-including them one within the other. This results in a complete array of forty-nine units of rectification such as we achieve during the forty-nine days of counting the Omer between Pesach and Shavuot. The fiftieth unit represents the source of the emotive powers in *binah*, which comprises fifty "gates."[11]

There are many synonyms for "joy" in Hebrew, one of which is *chedvah* (חֶדְוָה). *Chedvah* relates to an initial, sharp peak of joy in the soul that sends shivers through one's flesh.[12] This is similar to an initial sense of awe or fear that similarly gives us "goosebumps." *Chedvah* thus reflects the union between rectified fear of God and pure joy.

Modern medicine acknowledges that happiness in life bolsters our immune system and its ability to defend us against invaders. Being joyful improves our health. The *Chedvah* Breathing Meditation[13] is an authentic Jewish breathing method that fosters the initial, piercing sense of joy through controlled breathing. Studying this meditation will help us reinforce our faith in the one God, Who continuously resuscitates us with the breath of life.

---

11. See our book in Hebrew, *Esa Einai* pp. 161-167.
12. See Rashi on Exodus 18:9.
13. See Appendix.

2

ZEBULUN, WALKING AND HEALING

Health authorities have determined that those who have interacted with an infected individual should self-quarantine for fourteen days. While at home in quarantine for this fortnight, we have ample time for intellectual meditation. An appropriate idea would be to meditate each day on one of the fourteen complementary pairs of times that appear in Ecclesiastes.[1]

In this chapter, King Solomon enumerates twenty-eight changing times, listed in fourteen pairs. Each "time" marks a phase of human experience and endeavor in this world. In Kabbalah, these phases correspond to the twenty-eight phases of the moon in its monthly cycle around the earth.

The fourteen pairs also correspond to the first fourteen days of the month of Nisan. During the first days of Nisan, each tribe brought an inauguration offering to the *Mishkan*, the Tabernacle, in the desert.

---

1. Ecclesiastes ch. 3.

Here, we will suggest a meditation on the third pair, "A time to kill and a time to heal."[2]

The first twelve of these fourteen pairs correspond to each of the tribes. The tribe that brought the offering on the third day, corresponding to "A time to kill and a time to heal," is the tribe of Zebulun. According to the great Kabbalist the Arizal, the origin of the soul of this tribe corresponds to *keter* (the *sefirah* of crown), the superconscious source of respiration that relates to faith in God.

"A time to kill" appears to be the most negative of all the times. In contrast, "A time to heal" appears to be a constructive time that brings healing to the world. Yet, this phrase corresponds to the righteous tribe of Zebulun, how can we attribute to them "a time to kill"?

The tribe of Zebulun did not spend their time studying Torah all day. They dealt with worldly matters, traveling overseas to do business. With the income they received from their trade, they would supply the tribe of Issachar with all they needed to sit and study Torah. Zebulun observed the teaching in the *Mishnah*, "All your dealings should be for the sake of heaven."[3]

The Alter Rebbe, in his seminal work, the Tanya,[4] defines three types of individuals: one who is wicked, one who is intermediate and one who is righteous, i.e., one who has overcome his evil inclination. The righteous

---

2.   Ibid vs. 3.
3.   *Pirkei Avot* 2:12.
4.   Tanya ch. 1.

type divides further into two categories: the incomplete *tzadik* and the complete *tzadik*. The incomplete *tzadik* has not yet completely overcome his evil inclination. However, his tendency towards evil is suppressed in his unconscious mind and does not interfere with his service of God.

The complete *tzadik* has killed his evil inclination until it no long troubles him. King David attested that he achieved this level, saying, "My heart is hollow inside me."[5] The Alter Rebbe wrote of this verse, "He killed it [the evil inclination] through fasting." King David repented with such a strong will that he succeeded in completely overcoming his evil inclination.

Yet, there is an even higher level of the complete *tzadik*. Once he has killed the evil inclination, he heals it so that it no longer tempts him to do evil. Instead, it assists him in doing good and perfecting his deeds. In its healed state, the evil inclination is "very good."[6] The Zohar,[7] states, "Turning darkness into light and bitter tastes into sweetness." In this way, the complete *tzadik* serves God with "all his heart,"[8] i.e., with both his good and evil inclinations.[9] This is how in the verse from Ecclesiastes, the power to kill is associated with the power to heal.

Of the twenty-eight times, "a time to heal" relates to

5.   Psalms 109:22.

6.   Genesis 1:34.

7.   *Zohar Bereishit* 4a.

8.   See Deuteronomy 6:5.

9.   Ibid, Rashi ad loc.

the physician. The letters that spell the phrase, "and a time to heal" (וְעֵת לִרְפּוֹא) permute to spell the phrase, "an act of light" (פְּעוּלַת אוֹר). The power of the physician to heal begins by projecting a comforting light to his patient.

At the onset of creation, God began healing the shattered World of Chaos by creating good light. The mundane world we live in is the World of Rectification. It is incumbent on us to repair a world that was shattered by sin by infusing it with the healing light of *teshuvah*.

Of the twenty-eight times, "a time to heal" is the sixth from the beginning and the twenty-third from the end. This alludes to the verse, "And God said, 'Let there be light,' and there was light" (וַיֹּאמֶר אֱ־לֹהִים יְהִי אוֹר וַיְהִי אוֹר), which comprises six words and twenty-three letters.[10]

The Book of Formation, attributed to Abraham, the first Jew, enumerates twelve senses of the soul. Each sense corresponds to one of the tribes. The sense of the tribe of Zebulun is walking. The tribe of Zebulun were seafarers, always on the go. They collected precious gems from overseas.

Moses blessed the tribe of Zebulun: "And to Zebulun he said, 'Rejoice, Zebulun, in your departure, and Yissachar, in your tents." "Departure" refers to commerce, and "tents" refers to studying in the tents of Torah. Yet, rather than using their business acumen to accumulate great

---

10. "Healing" (רְפוּאָה) permutes to spell "the light of the mouth" (אוֹר פֶּה). The numerical value of this phrase is 292, which is also the numerical value of, "the light of circumcision" (אוֹר מִילָה). See our book, *Body Mind and Soul*, pp. 251-252.

wealth, the men from the tribe of Zebulun healed their wanderlust and profit-seeking by sharing the wealth acquired from their voyages with their brother tribe, Issachar, who spent their time studying Torah.[11]

Supporting a Torah scholar financially is a commendable act of charity. The numerical value of the phrase, "Indeed, charity is for life"[12] (כֵּן צְדָקָה לְחַיִּים) is 367, which is the numerical value of "corona" (קוֹרוֹנָה),[13] suggesting that giving charity is a spiritual antidote for this physical ailment. This idea is upheld by two verses in Proverbs that end with the phrase, "charity will save from death."[14] Like Zebulun, we can increase our merits by increasing our charity-giving. Charity, corresponding to *chesed* (the *sefirah* of lovingkindness), also encompasses performing acts of kindness, reaching out and helping others in need whenever possible.

In commanding us to follow the precepts of Jewish

---

11. For more about the relationship between Issachar and Zebulun, see our book, *The Inner Dimension*, pp. 387-392.

12. Proverbs 11:19

13. There are several phrases that have a numerical value of 367. Some others are mentioned later in this booklet. Each phrase alludes to a different *mitzvah* that can spiritually shield us from the virus that is causing the current pandemic. See our article *Corona: Chassidic Health Guidelines*, https://www.inner.org/torah_and_science/torah-healing/corona-chassidic-health-guidelines.

    Two more of these correspondences are the numerical value of "sound mind" (שֵׂכֶל טוֹב) and the short request that Moses prayed when his sister Miriam suffered from the spiritual malady of *tzara'at*: "please heal her" (רְפָא נָא לָהּ).

14. Proverbs 10:2; 11:4.

law, *halachah* (הֲלָכָה), God urges us not to be standers, but to be constantly "walking" (הֲלִיכָה) i.e., to progress in the service of God. As Zebulun did in his travels, God wishes us to discover the spiritual sparks buried in the mundane world and to redeem them. While confined to our homes and immediate neighborhoods, we can maintain this mindset of supporting Torah scholars, helping others in need, and constantly progressing in our service of God, thus extracting more holiness from our mundane lives.

When we walk, we employ both legs. In the teachings of Kabbalah, the right leg is associated with *netzach* (the *sefirah* of victory) and the left leg with *hod* (the *sefirah* of acknowledgment).

The inner dimension of *netzach* is confidence. One great Talmudic sage who demonstrated great confidence in God was Nachum Ish Gamzu. The numerical value of his name (אִישׁ גַּם זוּ) is also 367, the numerical value of the name of the virus, as mentioned. He asserted about whatever happened, "This too [גַּם זוּ] is for good." The following anecdote from the Talmud,[15] illustrates the power of this saying:

> *Once, the Jews desired to send the Emperor a gift. After discussing who should go, they decided that Nachum of Gamzu should go because he had experienced many miracles. They sent with him a bag full of precious stones and pearls. He went and spent the night in a certain inn and during the night the people in the inn arose and emptied*

---

15. *Ta'anit* 21a; Jerusalem Talmud, *Shekalim* 5:4.

the bag and filled it with earth. When he discovered this next morning he exclaimed, "This too is for the best!" When he arrived at his destination and they undid his bag they found that it was full of earth. The king thereupon desired to put them all to death claiming, "The Jews are mocking me!" Nachum then exclaimed, "This too is for the best!" Whereupon Elijah appeared in the guise of one of them and remarked, "Perhaps this is some of the earth of their father Abraham, for when he threw earth [against the enemy] it turned into swords and when [he threw] stubble it changed into arrows, for it is written, 'His sword makes them as dust, his bow as the driven stubble.'"[16]

There was one province which [the emperor had] not been able to conquer but when they tried some of this earth [against it] they were able to conquer it. Then they took him [Nachum] to the royal treasury and filled his bag with precious stones and pearls and sent him back with great honor.

On his return journey he again spent the night in the same inn. There, they asked him, "What did you take [to the king] that they showed you such great honor?" He replied, "I brought what I had taken from here." [The innkeepers] then razed the inn to the ground and took of the earth to the king and they said to him, "The earth that was brought to you belonged to us." They tested it and it was not found to be [effective] and the innkeepers were put to death.

---

16. Isaiah 41:2.

Nachum had great confidence in the need to stride ahead no matter what confronted him. His confidence stemmed from his belief that "this too is for the best."

Netzach corresponds to the endocrine system which activates the hormones in the body. The endocrine and the immune systems work together to ensure optimal growth, functionality and sustained health. In the physiological systems, *hod* (the *sefirah* of acknowledgment) corresponds to the immune system.

Hod further corresponds to the left leg. The inner dimension of *hod* is sincerity, which relates to passive trust. To be sincere in our trust in God, we must first acknowledge ourselves – identify ourselves and distinguish ourselves from foreign elements. This is the basic function of the immune system. In order to identify and fight against invading pathogens and infected cells, the body must first be able to identify itself. This enables it to eliminate the foe. An unstable immune system may begin to fight against the body's own healthy cells. This phenomenon manifests in auto-immune diseases.

The tribe of Zebulun corresponds to the left leg, which steps out first when we begin to walk, as we learn from the verse, "He who steps out with sincerity [the quality associated with *hod*], will walk with confidence [the quality associated with *netzach*]."[17] Therefore, Zebulun also corresponds to the immune system, which ensures our continued health.

---

17. Proverbs 10:9.

The Way the Immune System Works and its Spiritual Root

Most prospective pathogens are blocked by physical barriers in the body, such as the skin, mucus, etc. The immune system fights foreign elements that bypass the physical barriers in two stages. When a pathogen, such as a bacteria or virus, enters the system, the innate immune system identifies it and aims to eliminate it. If this first response does not overcome the threat, cells from the innate system produce specific antigens that signal the adaptive, or acquired, immune system to step in.

The ability of the immune system to kill or heal manifests in the types of cells it produces. When a pathogen invades the body, the first cells to go into action are white blood cells called macrophages. A healthy individual may have up to 10^{10} macrophages patrolling the bloodstream for invaders. Macrophages are divided into two general categories: M1 and M2. These cells either attack infected cells and kill them or consume pathogens and other debris that accumulates as a result of cell decay. M1 macrophages **kill** (infectious organisms, virus-infected cells, or malignant cells) and M2 macrophages **heal** (sterile wounds and, with less success, tumors). This is the initial stage of action of the innate immune system.

If this first line of strategy is unsuccessful, the antigens produced by the innate immune system trigger the adaptive immune system to produce other white blood cells. B cells develop a unique antibody that kills the specific pathogen. Other white blood cells produced by the adaptive immune system are Th cells. Th1 lymphocytes activate antigen-specific macrophages, while Th2 immune responses inhibit macrophage activation. Once again, these cells can either kill or heal. Researchers have noticed that a Th2-like response causes the infected species to ultimately succumb to infection. In contrast, in animals with the Th1 response the infection is healed.

In Kabbalah, the root of the paradoxical power of the immune system to kill or heal stems from *keter* (the *sefirah* of crown), which bears contradictory states simultaneously. *Keter* lies at the top of the middle axis of the *sefirot*. Unlike all the other *sefirot* which tend either to the right or to the left, the Zohar states that in *keter* there is no left, it is all right.[18] This is because the mighty force of the left is included in the right, and instead of opposing it, empowers it. Like a circular crown spinning clockwise above the head, in *keter*, right and left are indistinguishable. Indeed, *keter* is our fortune, like a ball spinning on a roulette wheel, we can never be aware of what it will bring us next.

It also reflects the essence of *keter* to bear paradoxes. When the ball drops into place, you either lose or you win. Yet, until the ball drops, it is in superposition, bearing both qualities simultaneously. When the ball

---

18. *Zohar Shemot* 129a. For more on this idea see our book, *The Inner Dimension, Parashat Korach* (an English version will soon be available, *be"H*).

finally lands in *hod*, at once there is a loser and a winner. The Zohar describes this phenomenon in its interpretation of the verse, "and God shall plague Egypt, plaguing and healing,"[19] "plaguing Egypt and healing Israel,"[20] simultaneously.

The sum of the numerical values of the two Hebrew roots, "plaguing" (נ־ג־ף) and "healing" (ר־פ־א) is 414, which equals two times "light" (אוֹר), as in the abovementioned verse, "And God said, 'Let there be light!' and there was light." The root of "light" (א־ר) is also the two-lettered root of "cursed" (אָרוּר). The very same light that heals the sick, also metes out punishment on the wicked.

A similar manifestation of the same paradoxical power was apparent at the Splitting of the Red Sea. The verse in the Song of the Sea states, "Your right hand, God, praised for its might; Your right hand, God, crushes the foe."[21] Rashi interprets,

> *When the Israelites perform the will of the Omnipresent, [even] the left hand becomes a right hand. The right hand, empowered with might, saves Israel, and … that very right hand [also] crushes the foe, unlike a human being, who cannot perform two kinds of work with the same hand.*

These two examples testify[22] to the paradoxical power of

---

19. Isaiah 19:22.
20. *Zohar Shemot* 36a.
21. Exodus 15:6.
22. The numerical values of the two roots, "plague" (נ־ג־ף) and "healing" (ר־פ־א) are 133 and 281, respectively. Their average value is 207,

the Almighty to achieve two opposite deeds at the same time.

Hod (the *sefirah* of acknowledgment) is the final *sefirah* on the left. It is the most left of the left. From this point on, one can either continue to live by turning right, towards *yesod*, by acknowledging God's lovingkindness (similar to the Th1 response), or, God-forbid, one turns to the opposite of life and rebels against His infinite grace (the Th2 response). Thus, of all the *sefirot*, *hod* is the most conscious of the ability of *keter* to bear paradoxes. In *hod* (הוֹד), either I acknowledge my faith in God, by thanking Him for all that transpires, or God-forbid "my complexion [הוֹדִי] was turned in me into corruption."[23] These two outcomes depend on whether our general tendency is to attack the evil that we see in our lives (like M1 macrophages) or shine a positive, hopeful and healing light towards the pain we encounter (M2 macrophages).

---

which is the numerical value of "light" (אוֹר), as mentioned. This means that the wing on either side between the original numbers and their average is 74, which is the numerical value of "witness" (עֵד).

23. Daniel 10:8.

3

STRENGTHENING THE IMMUNE SYSTEM

The first thing we say when we wake up in the morning is the *Modeh Ani* prayer: "I offer thanks to You, living and eternal King, for having mercifully restored my soul within me; Your faithfulness is abundant." While we sleep, the soul leaves the body to refresh itself in the upper worlds. By saying this short prayer as we awake, we offer thanks to God for restoring our soul to our body in the morning.

God does not only vitalize us when we awaken every morning. With every breath we take, He infuses us with new life.[1] It is incumbent upon us to be eternally grateful to Him.

Kabbalah teaches us that God vitalizes the world through ten channels of Divine energy or life force, called *sefirot* (sing., *sefirah*). The eighth *sefirah* is *hod* (the *sefirah* of acknowledgment).[2] *Hod* (הוד) relates to

---

1. See *Bereishit Rabah* 14:9.
2. The complete array of ten *sefirot* is: *keter* (the *sefirah* of crown), *chochmah* (the *sefirah* of wisdom), *binah* (the *sefirah* of understanding), *chesed* (the *sefirah* of lovingkindness), *gevurah* (the *sefirah* of

29

"thanksgiving" (הוֹדָיָה), "acknowledgment" (הוֹדָאָה) and "confession" (וִדּוּי).

Chassidut teaches us that each *sefirah* manifests in the human psyche via a different quality. The *sefirah* of *hod* is demonstrated through wholehearted sincerity. The forbidden forms of sorcery and witchcraft mentioned in the Torah are the antithesis to this attribute.[3] After listing these forbidden practices, the Torah concludes with the verse, "Be wholehearted with God, your God."[4]

The famous medieval Biblical commentator, Rashi, explained this verse as follows:

> *"Walk with God in simplicity, wait for Him, and do not delve into the future, but rather all of life's events should be accepted with simplicity, and then you will be with Him and in His portion.*[5]

Sincerity means refraining from using foreign methods to divine the future. It also implies honesty in all one's social transactions.

As mentioned, in human physiology, *hod* corresponds

---

might), *tiferet* (the *sefirah* of beauty), *netzach* (the *sefirah* of victory), *hod* (the *sefirah* of acknowledgment), *yesod* (the *sefirah* of foundation) and *malchut* (the *sefirah* of kingdom). In some cases, *da'at* (the *sefirah* of knowledge), is included after *chochmah* and *binah*, in place of *keter*.

3.   For more on this topic, see the article, *The Importance of Being Earnest (Part 1):* on our website www.inner.org. https://www.inner.org/wp-content/uploads/2014/02/E65-1206-1.pdf

4.   Deuteronomy 18:13.

5.   Rashi ad. loc.

to the immune system.[6] To strengthen our immune system, we should cultivate a sense of gratitude to those who are benevolent to us and acknowledge our indebtedness to others for their physical and spiritual gifts. For example, we must acknowledge the truth of another's words and thank him for enlightening us and correcting our mistakes. By sincerely acknowledging our indebtedness to others, we transcend our egocentric subjectivity. This cultivates in us the objectivity necessary to distinguish between an ally or an adversary. We are thus able to connect to a friend or repel a foe, both on the spiritual and physical planes.

Hod (the *sefirah* of acknowledgment) exudes from *binah* (the *sefirah* of understanding), whose inner experience is joy. Gratitude to God stems from reaping happiness from all that God sends our way.

---

6.   See our book, *Body, Mind and Soul* p. 86.

4

THE *CHEDVAH* BREATHING MEDITATION

As mentioned, in the physiological systems, the respiratory system corresponds to *keter* (the *sefirah* of crown). Respiration is the physical conduit through which the spirit of life enters the body. In breathing, we inhale that which is above us, internalizing that which is exterior to us.[1]

In Hebrew, "inhaling" (שְׁאִיפָה) also means "aspiration." Breathing is an expression of the soul's innate desire to ascend beyond its conscious self into the realm of the superconscious. *Keter* is our superconscious link to God, where our souls remain eternally connected to the Divine.

All physical phenomena are rooted in the spiritual realm. Thus, when we feel unwell, while following doctors' orders on the physical level, we must also seek to heal the spiritual root of our ailment.

Since the respiratory system corresponds to *keter*, which includes the powers of faith, spiritual pleasure and will, breathing dysfunctions may indicate a lack of faith in the Divine purpose that infuses creation, or the absence of the Divine as a source of pleasure and motivation in life.

---

1. See our book, *Body, Mind, and Soul* p. 85.

On the other hand, proper respiration and healthy lungs help us strengthen our faith in God, renew our pleasure in life and reinforce our will to live a productive life. All this is especially relevant regarding the current virus and the spiritual aspect of curing respiratory ailments.

While we breathe, we should have in mind to connect to God. This helps us consciously integrate the vitality that He blesses us with at every living moment. We should become conscious that we are inhaling into our being new inspiration to live and become motivated by a new sense of pleasure and purpose.

In Hebrew, there are ten different synonyms for "joy."[2] Relative to the three other most common synonyms,[3]

---

2. *Shir Hashirim Rabah* 1:5.
3. The four most common synonyms for "joy" and their correspondences:

Synonym for "joy"	The four letters of Havayah	The *sefirot*	Type of joy	Synonym in Hebrew
chedvah	י	*Chochmah* (the *sefirah* of wisdom)	Initial sharp sense of joy	חֶדְוָה
gilah	ה	*Binah* (the *sefirah* of understanding)	Concealed joy that fills the heart	גִּילָה
simchah	ו	The six *midot* from *chesed* (the *sefirah* of lovingkindness) to *yesod* (the *sefirah* of foundation)	Joy that bursts out, expressed through clapping, dance and song, etc.	שִׂמְחָה
sasson	ה	*Malchut* (the *sefirah* of kingdom)	The ecstatic peak of joy	שָׂשׂוֹן

chedvah corresponds to the letter *yud* of God's essential Name, *Havayah*, which is the origin of all the other letters of the Name. *Chedvah* is thus the source of joy that stems from a very high level of the soul. As mentioned in the Introduction, *chedvah* relates to an initial, sharp peak of joy in the soul that sends shivers through one's flesh.[4] It is the cutting-edge of joy that generates all other levels of joy in the soul, to allow us to "serve God with joy,"[5] while simultaneously serving God with fear. We can integrate the joy of *chedvah* into our being with every breath we take.

The four letters of *chedvah* (חֶדְוָה) correspond to the four stages of meditative breathing: inhaling, holding the breath, exhaling and resting. In the *sefirot*, these correspond to the will of *keter* and the three intellectual faculties of the soul, *chochmah* (the *sefirah* of wisdom), *da'at* (the *sefirah* of knowledge) and *binah* (the *sefirah* of understanding).[6]

---

4.   See Rashi on Exodus 18:9.

5.   Psalms 100:2.

6.   The Name of God that appears in the abovementioned interpretation of the verse, "With every breath, praise God," is *Kah* (יה). Relative to the other Names of God, *Kah* corresponds to *chochmah* (the *sefirah* of wisdom) and to the letter *yud* of the Tetragrammaton. In greater detail, the *yud* and the *hei* allude to all four *sefirot* from *keter* to *da'at*: the tip of the *yud* corresponds to *keter* (the *sefirah* of crown), the body of the *yud* to *chochmah* (the *sefirah* of wisdom), and the lower pathway of the *yud* corresponds to *da'at* (the *sefirah* of knowledge). The letter *hei* corresponds to *binah* (the *sefirah* of understanding). These four *sefirot* correspond to the four stages of breathing, as explained in the text.

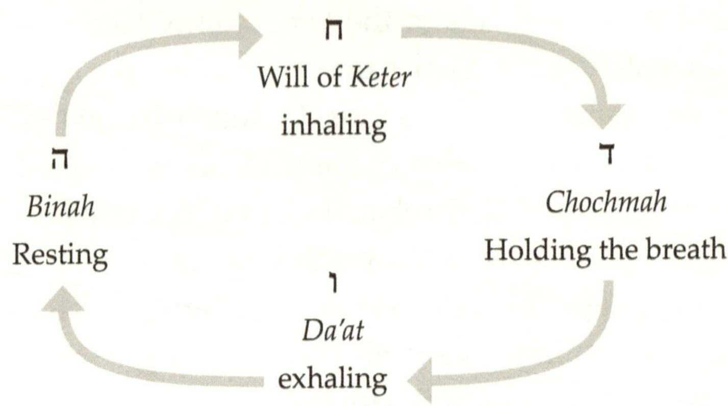

The *Chedvah* Breathing Cycle

The name of the initial letter of *chedvah* is *chet* (ח),[7] corresponding to the first stage of inhaling new air into the lungs. The name of the letter *chet* (חֵית) relates to both "vitality" (חַיּוּת), and "fear" (as in the phrase חִתַּת אֱ־לֹהִים "the fear of God"[8]). Life and fear are related, as the verse states, "Fear of God to [i.e., is the source of] life."[9] The initial experience of life is a sharp point of fear. This reflects the original "shock" of "becoming alive."

The second letter of *chedvah* is *dalet* (ד),[10] which corresponds to the stage of holding the breath. The name of this letter (דָּלֶת) is conjugate to "poverty" (דַּלּוּת). The form of the *dalet*, is like a bent-over human figure. The *dalet* thus symbolizes a state of "selflessness" or "self-nullification." This is the inner experience of *chochmah* (the

---

7.   See our book, *The Hebrew Letters, Chet*.

8.   Genesis 35:5.

9.   Proverbs 19:23.

10. See our book *The Hebrew Letters, Dalet*

sefirah of wisdom). While holding the breath in our lungs, we nullify ourselves to the Divine life-giving force inherent in the air that we have inhaled, realizing that like a pauper who cannot survive without charitable gifts from others, without the Divine gift of breath, we would not be alive. Holding the breath is bringing the superconscious experience into the conscious mind.

The third letter of *chedvah* is a *vav* (ו).[11] The essence of the letter *vav* is connection. As we exhale the air that we have breathed in, we bring the breath into our bodies, drawing the truth of our connection to God into each limb.

Resting is the final stage of the breathing cycle, which corresponds to the letter *hei* (ה)[12] of *chedvah* and the mother principle of *binah* (the *sefirah* of understanding). Like a child who comes to rest for a moment in his mother's embrace before running off to play again, once the consciousness of God has reached its location in every part of the body, we allow it to integrate into our being while we rest before taking the next breath. *Binah* further corresponds to the World to Come, the world of eternal rest.

After resting, we begin the cycle with a new aspiration. We inhale a new breath, representing our renewed desire to experience a new phase of life. With every breath we take we receive a new inspiration.

---

11. See ibid., *Vav.*
12. See ibid., *Hei.*

5

FINDING JOY IN BREATHING – THE *CHEDVAH* BREATHING TECHNIQUE

In order to correlate the breathing cycle to the secret of the word *chedvah*, and initiate the sharp state of joy, which generates all the other levels of happiness in our souls, we translate the four letters of this word into their numerical values.

As mentioned, the letters of *chedvah* (חֶדְוָה) are *chet* (ח), *dalet* (ד), *vav* (ו) and *hei* (ה). The corresponding numerical values of these four letters are 8, 4, 6 and 5, respectively. This is the rhythm that we count as we breathe, meditating on the letters at each stage.

- *Chet* (ח): Inhale for a count of 8
- *Dalet* (ד): Hold for a count of 4:
- *Vav* (ו): Exhale for a count of 6
- *Hei* (ה): Rest for a count of 5:

After we have repeated the exercise several times, this breathing cycle will become more natural, until it will no longer be necessary to consciously count the pace. Once this happens, we can instead apply the intentions of many different verses of the Torah that reflect the same rhythm.[1]

The foremost verse that we can consider in this context is the verse of *Shema,* "Hear O' Israel, God is our God, God is one" (שְׁמַע יִשְׂרָאֵל הוי' אֱ-לֹהֵינוּ הוי' אֶחָד).

In this meditation, as we inhale, we have in mind the eight Hebrew letters of the first two words of this verse, "Hear O' Israel" (שְׁמַע יִשְׂרָאֵל).

As we hold the breath, we meditate on the four letters of God's essential Name, *Havayah* (י-הוה).

The next word "our God," (אֱ-לֹהֵינוּ), comprises six letters, corresponding to exhaling to the count of six.

The final stage of resting corresponds to the last two words of the verse, "God is one" (י-הוה אֶחָד). *Havayah* (י-הוה) has 4 letters and we relate to "one" as the numeral 1, completing a total of 5.

Thus, the entire phrase is *chedvah,* 8, 4, 6, 5. By meditating on this verse while breathing to this rhythm, God's oneness resonates through our souls and bodies, "God is one." In this way we breathe joy in our experience of uniting God in our souls and bodies: "Hear O' Israel, *Havayah* is our God, *Havayah* is one."

------

1. See our book in Hebrew, *Esa Einai* p. 180ff.

MORE BOOKS BY RABBI GINSBURGH

GENERAL

What You Need to Know About Kabbalah

190 pages

The Wondering Jew

Mystical Musings & Inspirational Insights

284 pages

The Inner Dimension

Insight into the Weekly Torah Portion

405 pages

Kabbalah and Meditation for the Nations

216 pages

The Hebrew Letters

Channels of Creative Consciousness

502 pages

SCIENCE AND MATHEMATICS

913: The Secret Wisdom of Genesis

160 pages

The Breath of Life

Torah, Intelligent Design and Evolution

186 pages

137: The Riddle of Creation

400 pages

Lectures on Torah and Modern Physics

184 pages

Wisdom: Integrating Torah and Science

216 pages

The Torah of Life

Nutrition + Nervous System

44 pages

LEADERSHIP

Awakening the Spark Within

Five Dynamics of Leadership that can Change the World

200 pages

Rectifying the State of Israel

230 pages

Raising a Jewish Family

Consciousness and Choice

Finding Your Soulmate
284 pages

The Mystery of Marriage

How to Find True Love and
Happiness in Married Life
500 pages

The Art of Education

Internalizing Ever-
New Horizons
302 pages

Psychology and Meditation

Anatomy of the Soul

144 pages

A Sense of the Supernatural

Interpretation of Dreams and
Paranormal Experiences
208 pages

Transforming Darkness into Light

Kabbalah and Psychology
192 pages

Frames of Mind

Motivation According
to Kabbalah
256 pages

Living in Divine Space

Kabbalah and Meditation
288 pages

Health and Youthfulness

Body, Mind and Soul

Kabbalah on Human
Physiology, Disease
and Healing
342 pages

The Twinkle in Your Eye

Kabbalistic Remedies for
Preserving Youth and Memory
202 pages

www.ingramcontent.com/pod-product-compliance
Lightning Source LLC
Chambersburg PA
CBHW020943160726
47993CB00007B/2914